Book 1
Grades K–2

Lollipop Logic

Bonnie Risby
& Robert K. Risby, II

Prufrock Press Inc.
Waco, Texas

Prufrock Press Inc.
P.O. Box 8813
Waco, TX 76714-8813
Phone: (800) 998-2208
Fax: (800) 240-0333
http://www.prufrock.com

Contents

About This Book

Lollipop Logic is designed to present critical thinking skills to young students who may not have mastered reading skills. In the past these skills have been reserved for much older students; however, there is nothing lacking in the development of very young students to prohibit introducing and nurturing these skills other than a degree of reading proficiency. *Lollipop Logic* is unique in that it combines problems involving deduction, analogies, relationships, sequencing, pattern decoding, inferencing, and criteria analyzing skills in a format designed to appeal to the youngster from pre-school through first grade without the reading barrier. As young children develop these thinking skills, expect to see them approach all materials with critical forethought.

To the Instructor

Lollipop Logic is the direct result of requests by educators for lessons presenting critical thinking skills in a format suitable for younger students. The instructor is indeed the most important element in making critical thinking skills work for younger students. It is the instructor's role not only to present the process but also to foster an atmosphere that encourages creative and critical thinking with an absence of a fear of failure. Since the thought process itself is more important than the answers provided in the back of the book, it is very important to discuss and compare methods of arriving at conclusions and to be tolerant of creative diversions from the norm. It is suggested that each new type of skill be presented and discussed and that sample problems be worked together before students are challenged to work independently.

Skills Presented in This Book

Relationships

In this section, students will be looking for ways that certain things relate to one another. Some of the relationships will be obvious; others will be more subtle. Students should be reminded to be flexible and creative and not to become alarmed when the relationship they define is different than one discovered by their neighbors. Exercises in this section should be completed before introducing analogies, as analogical thinking is based on being able to identify relationships.

Analogies

Analogies are comparisons between things based on similar characteristics. This section contains both figural and pictorial analogies that are very similar to the literal or verbal analogies undertaken by older students. Although first attempts may be awkward, young children usually catch on to analogies quite readily, find them challenging, and relate to them with the adventurousness of one learning a new sport. To solve the analogies, students must find the relationship between the first two items and then establish the same or a very similar relationship between a second pair of items that completes the analogy. It would be helpful to go through several examples together before beginning individual work.

Deduction

Deduction is a form of inferencing in which the conclusion follows from premises or statements of fact. Since we are targeting a non-reading population, we have endeavored to keep the clues extremely brief. Instructors should read the clues clearly, repeat them carefully, and then allow the learner adequate time to solve the problem by logically linking together all the facts.

Sequences

Sequencing problems require students to look at time relationships. Pictorial sequences presented here require young thinkers to look at a group of illustrations to determine the relationship before selecting the item that must come first, the one coming second, etc. They must study the illustrations to discover the relationship that dictates the sequence. They should always be encouraged to take care and to correct any error that would create subsequent errors in the sequencing pattern.

Inference

Inferencing is a broad area of logic. Inferencing involves reaching conclusions from gathered evidence. It means going from the known to the unknown and forming educated guesses based on either facts or premises. This book includes pictorial exercises to introduce students to inferential thinking. They must critically examine the pictorial evidence presented and proceed to the next logical step or to the conclusion that is required.

Pattern Decoding

Exercises in pattern decoding present a series of figures that represent a pattern. Students are to study the illustrations to discover the pattern. Once they have discovered the pattern, they are to select one other illustration that would come next in the pattern. There are several skills that come into play in these exercises. Students must be able to distinguish between the visual images, recognize the pattern that is presented and forecast what the next element in the sequence will be. If students encounter trouble in completing the pattern, it may be necessary to go back and review one or more aspects of this skill.

Criteria Analyzing

Criteria analyzing skills involve examining given information and reaching conclusions from gathered evidence. This process is very similar to one of the oldest logic arguments, syllogisms. Done entirely with pictures, the young thinkers are presented with two groups of items to carefully scrutinize and analyze. They know the following:

All members of group A are Z.
All members of group B are not Z.

Then they are presented new items to examine and determine whether or not they are Z.

The pictures in both groups are nonsensical. They do, however, establish valid relationships that will lead to and support a conclusion.

Teacher's Instructions

Sequential Synthesis — Lessons 1-8

Note: For all sequencing lessons, caution students against marking the blanks too quickly without careful consideration. Remind them that an error in an early step of the solution could cause subsequent errors.

■ **Lesson 1**

Preface this exercise in sequencing by explaining that someone is building a structure of blocks. Each picture represents a logical step that must either precede or follow another sequential step. Carefully explain that there is only one logically acceptable solution so that they must consider the order very carefully. Students should number the first step in the sequence 1, the second 2, and so on.

■ **Lesson 2**

Explain that the following pictures show pieces of a puzzle being put together. Ask students to carefully consider which picture comes first and place a number 1 in the blank by that picture. Place a 2 by the picture that comes second, etc. Be sure students realize that there is only one correct sequence.

■ **Lesson 3**

Preface this exercise in sequencing by explaining that a farmer is going to pick the pears from his pear tree and is going to place them in a basket. They will see six pictures representing the different stages of the picking. Carefully explain that there is only one logically acceptable solution so they must consider carefully the order of the pictures. Students should number the pictures in the order they think they will happen.

■ **Lesson 4**

Instruct the students that what they are about to see is six views of the same nest. There are several bird eggs in the nest almost ready to hatch, but the eggs will not all hatch at once. By carefully considering the pictures, students can determine whether each of the six pictures precedes or follows another picture in the sequence. Carefully explain that there is only one logically acceptable solution, so they must consider carefully the order of the pictures. Students should number the pictures in the order they think they will happen.

■ **Lesson 5**

Preface this exercise in sequencing by explaining that someone is in the process of carving a jack-o-lantern from a pumpkin. They will see six pictures representing progressive stages of the pumpkin carving. Carefully explain that there is only one logically acceptable solution so they must consider carefully the order of the pictures. Students should number the pictures in the order they think they will happen.

■ **Lesson 6**

Preface this exercise in sequencing by explaining that some children are building a snowman. They will see six pictures representing progressive stages of the snowman building. Carefully explain that there is only one logically acceptable solution so they must consider carefully the order of the pictures. Students should number the pictures in the order they think they will happen.

■ **Lesson 7**

Preface this exercise in sequencing by explaining that someone is filling six glasses from a pitcher of lemonade. The pictures they will see will represent the progressive stages of filling the glasses. Carefully explain that there is only one logically acceptable solution so they must consider carefully the order of the pictures. Students should number the pictures in the order they think they will happen.

■ **Lesson 8**

Explain to students that they are going to see several pictures showing cookies on a plate. The first picture will be numbered 1 for them, and the second will be numbered 2. Using the first two pictures as clues, they will be able to establish a pattern, and then by careful consideration, they will be able to order the remaining picture in the sequence.

Relationships — Lessons 9 - 16

■ **Lessons 9 - 12**

All lessons in this section have the same instructions. Read the following instructions to students.

Look at the first thing in the row, the thing that is in the small box. It has something in common with one of the three things in the big box next to it. It could be that they are the same shape, the same design, the same size, or are alike in some other way. Find the one that is most like the first picture and draw a circle around it.

■ **Lessons 13 - 16**

All lessons in this section have the same instructions. Read the following instructions to youngsters.

A group of things that belong together are in the box. Look at the items in this group carefully to determine what they have in common or why they belong together. Then look carefully at the items below the box and decide if they could belong with the items in the group. If they could belong to the group in the box, draw a circle around them. If they could not belong to the group, draw an X through them.

Analogies — Lessons 17 - 24

Analogies are comparisons between two sets of things. They compare features that are not always obvious. Approach these pictorial and figural analogies with very young learners by carefully examining and talking about the example given. Remember this is a completely new concept for these young individuals. Don't be discouraged by awkward first attempts. Also, remember it is the process itself that we want to instill, so working in groups or sharing as a class are good initial approaches.

- **Lessons 17 - 19**

  Read the following instructions to students.

  Look at the two things in the first box. Think about how they are related. Then look at the thing in the smaller box to the right. One of the three things to the right of the smaller box is related to this thing in the same way the first two things are related. Find the one thing that is related to the thing in the small box in the same way the first two things are related. Draw a circle around this thing.

- **Lessons 20 - 24**

  For each page say:

  Look at the first two pictures. Think about how they are related. Then look for the two pictures underneath the top two pictures that are related to each other in the same way. Circle the correct pair.

Deductive Reasoning — Lessons 25 - 31

The activities in this section are designed with the pre-reader in mind; however, listening comprehension is required. Also the youngster must be able to distinguish the four characters in the activity. The figures are labeled, but some learners may wish to color them or code them in some other manner. Read the problem and clues slowly and distinctly, pause to allow thinking, and re-read clues. This presentation can be repeated as many times as necessary. If students are working in pairs or small groups, allow them enough time to discuss their solutions. Have students draw a line from each character to the item they are correctly associated with.

- **Lesson 25 - Vegetable Soup**

  Mrs. Wilson's class brought vegetables to class to make soup. Rob, Tom, Pat, and Ann brought carrots, potatoes, onions, and celery. See if you can figure out who brought each vegetable. Draw a line connecting the vegetable and the person who brought it.
  Clues
  1. Rob and the boy who brought carrots ride the bus.
  2. Ann and the girl who brought celery also ride the bus.
  3. Ann did not bring the onions.

- **Lesson 26 - Rides**

  John, Ben, Meg, and Diane all said if they could ride on whatever thing they wanted that they would pick a sail boat, a hot-air balloon, a helicopter, and a fire engine. Listen to the clues before matching each person with the ride of their dreams.
  Clues
  1. John and the boy who wanted to ride the fire engine are friends.
  2. Diane and the girl who wanted to ride in the hot-air balloon are sisters of the two boys.
  3. John did not want to go sailing because he gets seasick.

- **Lesson 27 - Pets**

  Pete, Luke, Sara, and Jill each have a pet. The pets are a cat, a dog, a rabbit, and a fish. Listen carefully to the clues and then draw a line from each pet to the person it belongs to.
  Clues
  1. Pete and the boy with the dog often meet at the pet store.
  2. Sara and the girl with the fish buy their pet supplies at a different pet store than the boys.
  3. Pete is allergic to cats.

- ## Lesson 28 - Sharing Time

    Matt, Paul, Chrissy, and Amy each brought a different thing for sharing time. They brought a caterpillar, an acorn, a sea shell, and a horseshoe for show and tell. Listen carefully to the clues and then draw a line connecting each person with what they brought.
    Clues
    1. Paul and the boy who brought a caterpillar sit next to each other.
    2. The girl bringing the acorn and Chrissy love show and tell days.
    3. Chrissy did not bring the sea shell.

- ## Lesson 29 - Halloween Party

    Dan, Scott, Lisa, and Kate came to the Halloween party dressed in different costumes. They came as a pirate, a cowboy, Cinderella, and a witch. Listen carefully to the clues and then draw a line from each person to their costume.
    Clues
    1. Dan and the boy who came as a cowboy liked bobbing for apples.
    2. Kate and girl who came as a witch liked the pumpkin relay.
    3. Dan was not Cinderella.

- ## Lesson 30 - Thanksgiving Feast

    The class is having a Thanksgiving feast that they prepare entirely by themselves. Adam, Joe, Lauren, and Kristi are in groups that are preparing mashed potatoes, cranberry sauce, corn, and pumpkin pie. Listen carefully to the clues and then draw a line connecting each person with what they will help prepare.
    Clues
    1. Adam and the boy helping with the cranberry sauce are working at tables next to each other.
    2. Lauren and the girl helping make pumpkin pie agree that the room smells delicious.
    3. Adam is not making the mashed potatoes.

- ## Lesson 31- Snack Time

    Ron, Bob, Mary, and Sue brought different things for snack time. They brought a banana, an apple, raisins, and cookies. Listen carefully to the clues and then draw a line connecting each person with what they brought.
    Clues
    1. Ron and the boy with the apple sat together under a tree to eat their snacks.
    2. Mary and the girl who brought raisins remembered to wash their hands before snack time.
    3. Ron did not bring a banana.

Pattern Decoding — Lessons 32 - 39

All lessons in this section have the same instructions. Read the following instructions to the students
Note: Some items in the answer list may be used more than once and some may not be used at all.

Study the following patterns carefully. After you find the pattern, choose the item in the answer list that should come next. Draw a line connecting the pattern to the item in the list that should come next.

Inference: Lessons 40 - 49

■ **Lessons 40 - 41**

Read the following instructions to students.

The pictures below have a part that is missing. The missing parts are along the side of the page. Find the missing part of each picture. Draw a line between the picture and its missing section.

■ **Lessons 42 - 43**

Read the following instructions to students.

Each picture has a missing piece. Beside it are several pieces that could fit in the place of the missing piece. Only one piece will fit and complete the picture. Choose the correct missing piece. Draw a circle around it.

■ **Lessons 44 - 45**

Read the following instructions to students.

Below are some pieces to a puzzle. Some of the pieces are missing. By carefully examining the pieces below you can get an idea of the total picture. After you know what the puzzle represents, draw the picture on a separate piece of paper.

■ **Lessons 46 - 47**

Read the following instructions to students.

The left side shows several different pictures. On the right side there are more pictures. Each picture on the left side is related to a picture on the right side in some way. Draw a line between each picture on the left and a picture on the right that it is most related to or goes with.

■ **Lesson 48 - 49**

Read the following instructions for all lessons.

There are four different drawings on this page. The drawings show only part of a larger drawing. Look at this part carefully and see if you can guess what the whole picture would look like. Describe what you think this is a picture of.

Criteria Analyzing Skills — Lessons 50 - 52

■ **Lessons 50 - 52**

Read the following instructions, inserting the correct name for the figures.

Several species of new life forms have been discovered on the planet Volgongo. See if you can identify them. The top row shows things that are triops. (oggs/tiffs) The next row shows things that are not triops (oggs/tiffs). Look at the creatures on the bottom and decide if they are triops (oggs/tiffs) or not. If they are, draw a circle around them. If they are not, draw an X through them. Look back at the examples as often as you like.

Number these pictures to show the correct order.

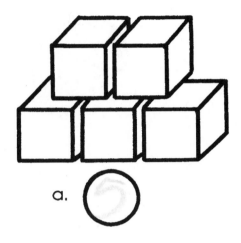

a.

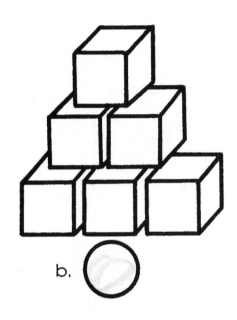

b.

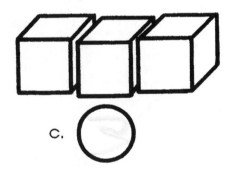

c.

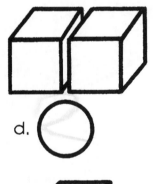

d.

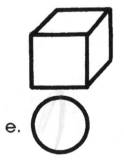

e.

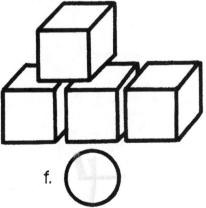

f.

Number these pictures to show the correct order.

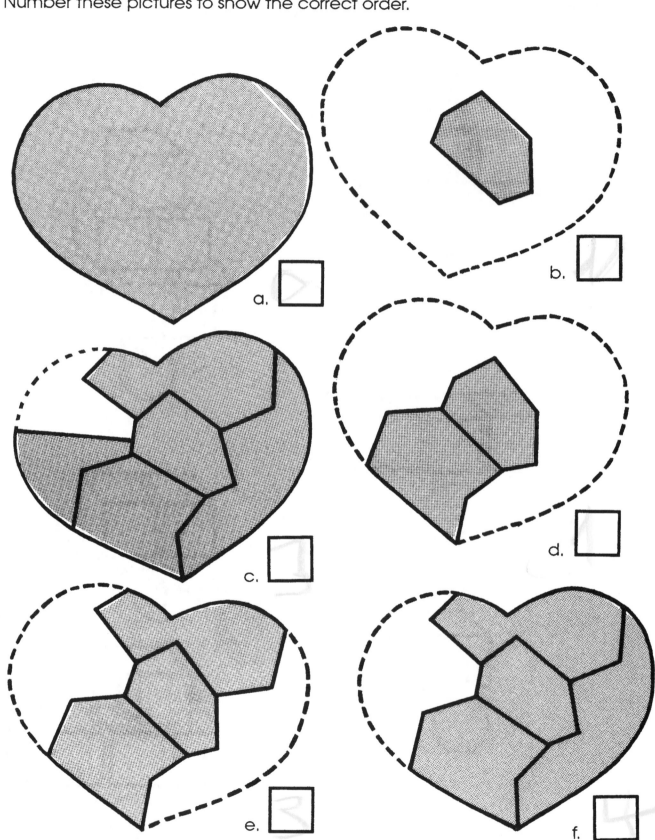

a.

b.

c.

d.

e.

f.

Number these pictures to show the correct order.

Number these pictures to show the correct order.

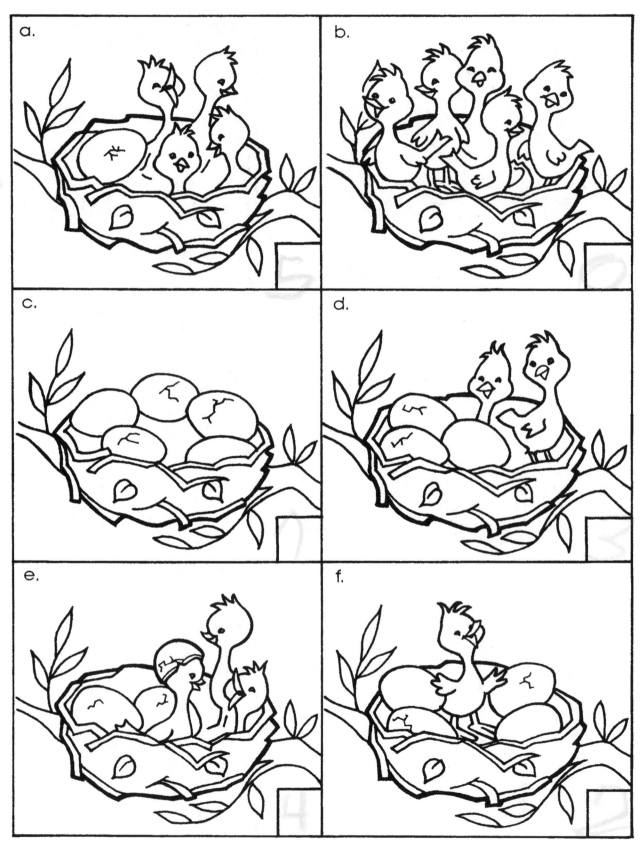

Number these pictures to show the correct order.

Number these pictures to show the correct order.

Number these pictures to show the correct order.

Number these pictures to show the correct order.

Draw a circle around the picture that has something in common with the first picture.

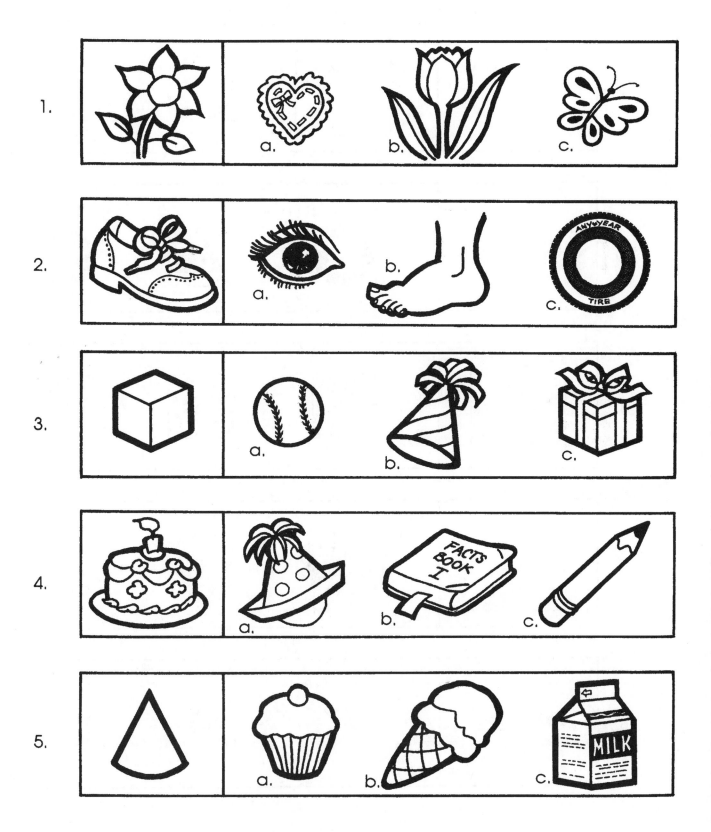

Draw a circle around the picture that has something in common with the first picture.

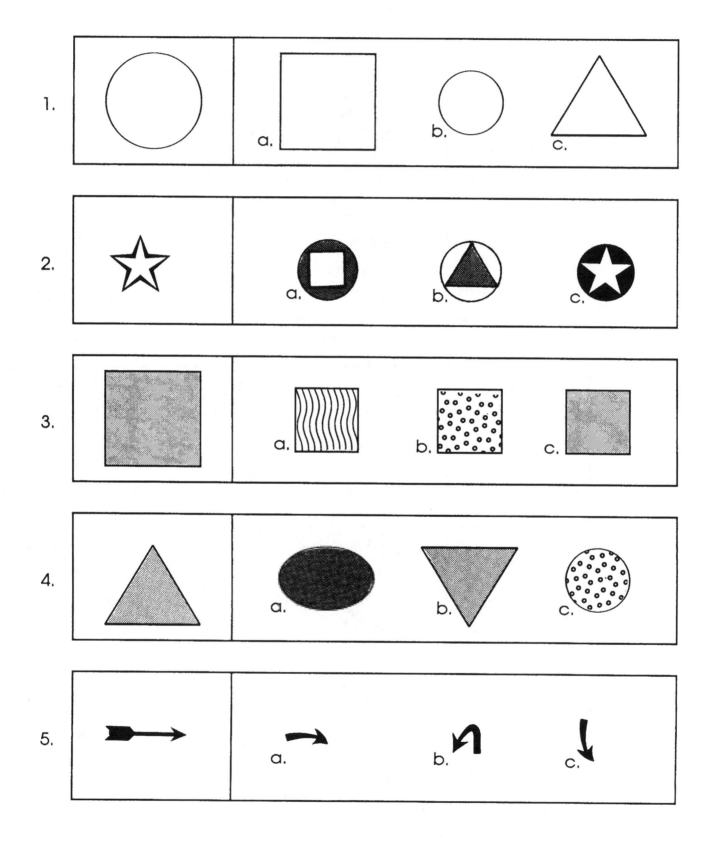

Draw a circle around the picture that has something in common with the first picture.

Draw a circle around the picture that has something in common with the first picture.

1.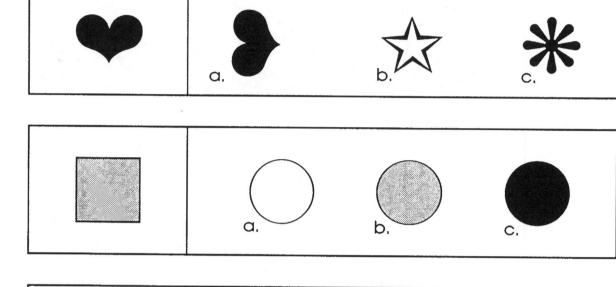

2.

3.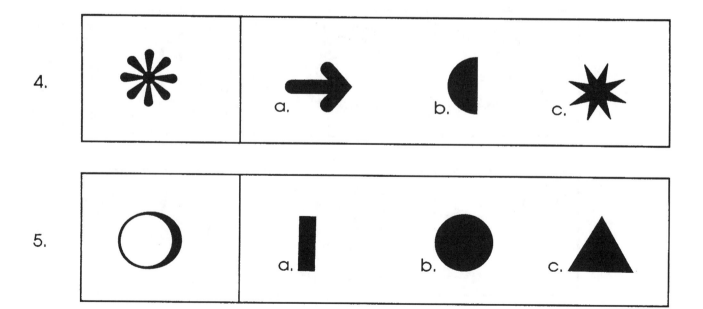

4.

5.

Circle the things on this page that belong in the group. Put an **X through** the things that do not belong in the group.

Circle the things on this page that belong in the group. Put an **X through** the things that do not belong in the group.

Circle the things on this page that belong in the group. Put an **X through** the things that do not belong in the group.

Circle the things on this page that belong in the group. Put an **X through** the things that do not belong in the group.

Circle the thing that is related to the third thing in the same way the first two things are related.

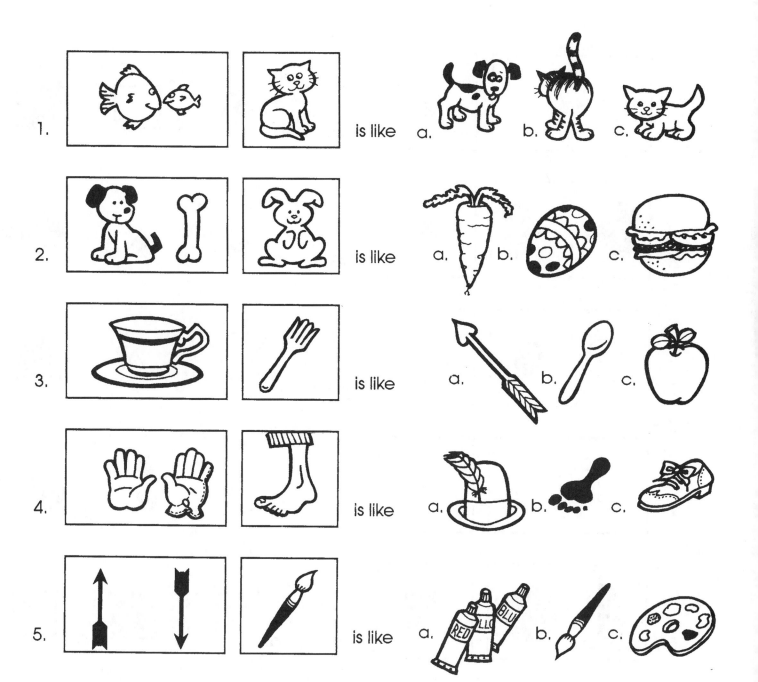

Lesson 18

Circle the thing that is related to the third thing in the same way the first two things are related.

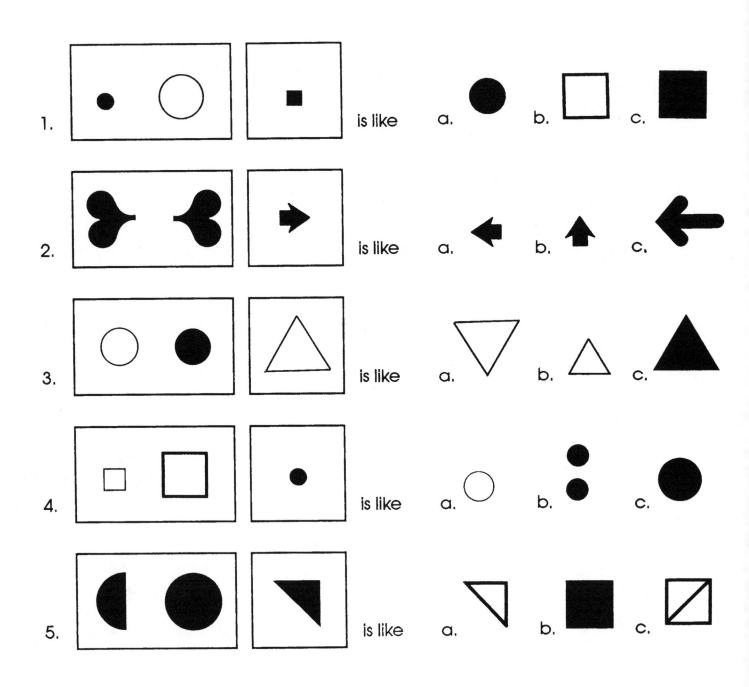

1. is like a. b. c.

2. is like a. b. c.

3. is like a. b. c.

4. is like a. b. c.

5. is like a. b. c.

Circle the thing that is related to the third thing in the same way the first two things are related.

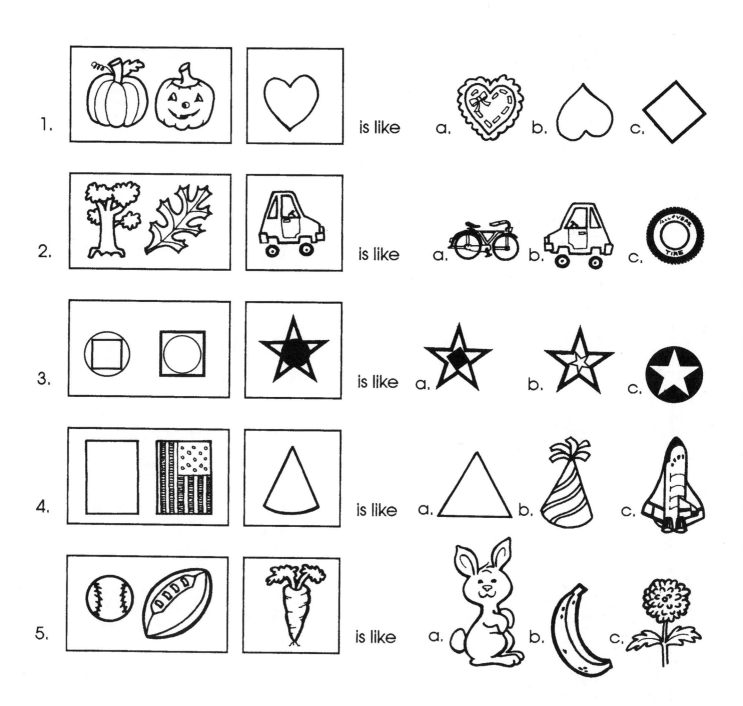

1. is like   a.   b.   c.

2. is like   a.   b.   c.

3. is like   a.   b.   c.

4. is like   a.   b.   c.

5. is like   a.   b.   c.

Choose the pair of pictures that are related to each other in the same way the top two pictures are related. Circle the correct pair.

Example: is like as is like

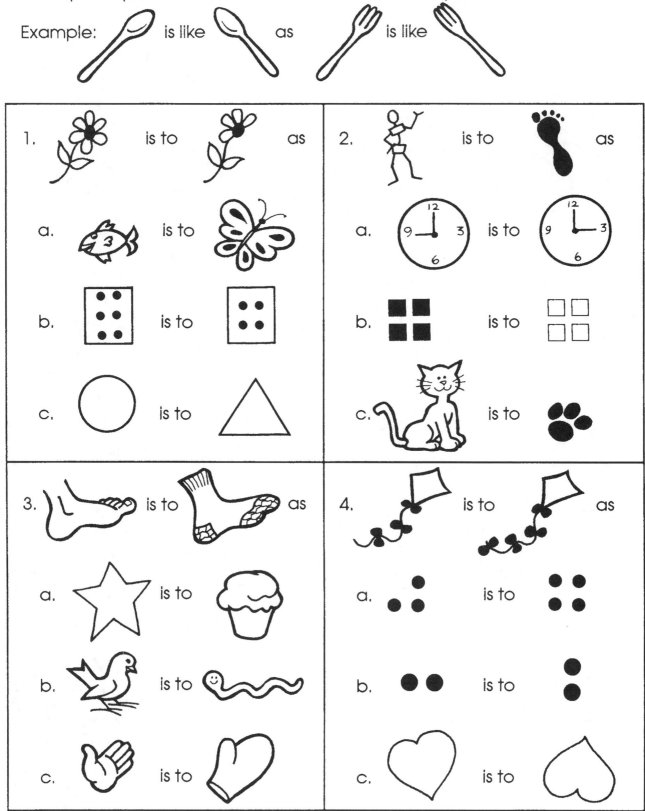

1. is to as

a. is to

b. is to

c. is to

2. is to as

a. is to

b. is to

c. is to

3. is to as

a. is to

b. is to

c. is to

4. is to as

a. is to

b. is to

c. is to

Choose the pair of pictures that are related to each other in the same way the top two pictures are related. Circle the correct pair.

Example   ☐ is like ■   as   ◯ is like ●

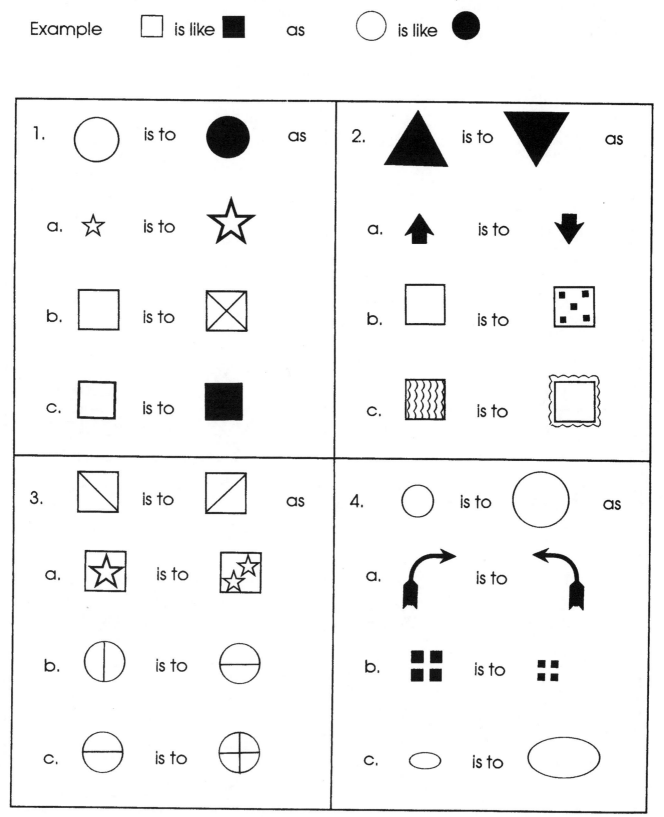

Choose the pair of pictures that are related to each other in the same way the top two pictures are related. Circle the correct pair.

Example:

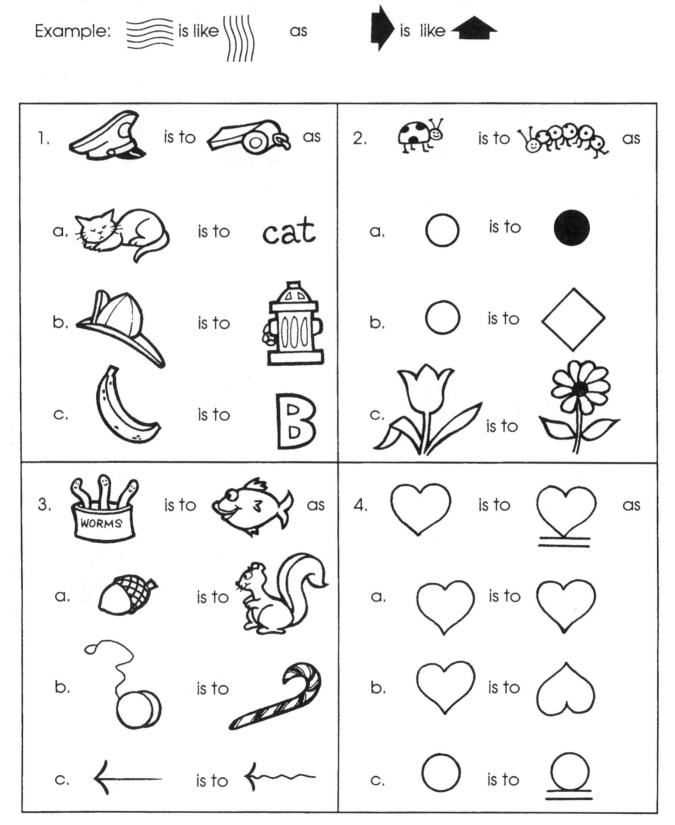

Choose the pair of pictures that are related to each other in the same way the top two pictures are related. Circle the correct pair.

Example:

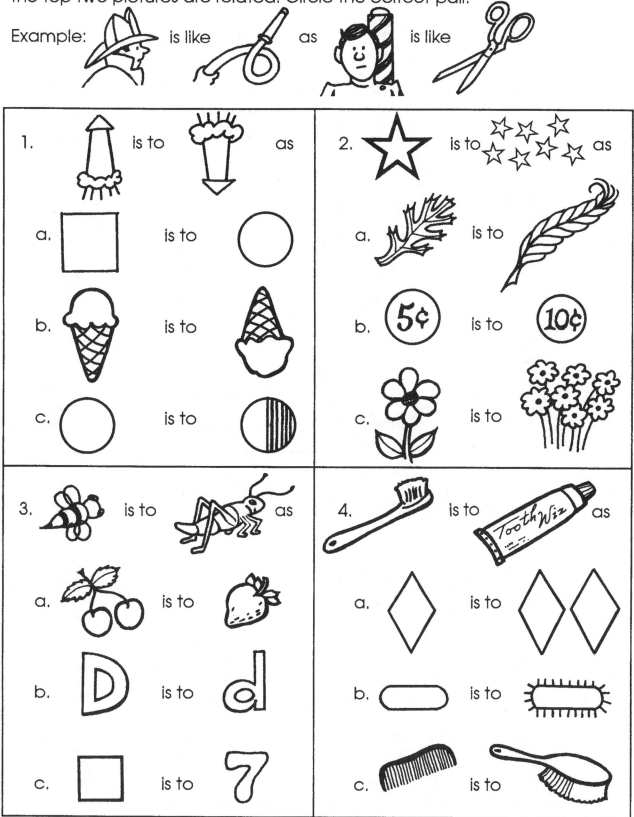

Choose the pair of pictures that are related to each other in the same way the top two pictures are related. Circle the correct pair.

Example:

Vegetable Soup

Mrs. Wilson's class brought vegetables to class to make soup. Rob, Tom, Pat, and Ann brought carrots, potatoes, onions, and celery. See if you can figure out who brought each vegetable. Draw a line connecting the vegetable and the person who brought it.

Clues

1. Rob and the boy who brought carrots ride the bus.
2. Ann and the girl who brought celery also ride the bus.
3. Ann did not bring the onions.

Rides

John, Ben, Meg, and Diane all said if they could pick a ride on whatever thing they wanted that they would pick a sail boat, a hot-air balloon, a helicopter, and a fire engine. Listen to the clues before matching each person with the ride of their dreams.

Clues

1. John and the boy who wanted to ride the fire engine are friends.

2. Diane and the girl who wanted to ride in the hot-air balloon are sisters.

3. John did not want to go sailing because he gets seasick.

Pets

Pete, Luke, Sara, and Jill each have a pet. The pets are a cat, a dog, a rabbit, and a fish. Listen carefully to the clues and then draw a line from each pet to the person it belongs to.

Clues

1. Pete and the boy with the dog often meet at the pet store.

2. Sara and the girl with the fish buy their pet supplies at a different pet store than the boys.

3. Pete is allergic to cats.

Sharing Time

Matt, Paul, Chrissy, and Amy each brought a different thing for sharing time. They brought a caterpillar, an acorn, a sea shell, and a horseshoe for show and tell. Listen carefully to the clues and then draw a line connecting each person with what they brought.

Clues

1. Paul and the boy who brought a caterpillar sit next to each other.
2. The girl bringing the acorn and Chrissy love show and tell days.
3. Chrissy did not bring the sea shell.

Halloween Party

Dan, Scott, Lisa, and Kate came to the Halloween party dressed in different costumes. They came as a pirate, a cowboy, Cinderella, and a witch. Listen carefully to the clues and then draw a line from each person to their costume.

Clues

1. Dan and the boy who came as a cowboy liked bobbing for apples.

2. Kate and girl who came as a witch liked the pumpkin relay.

3. Dan was not Cinderella.

Thanksgiving Feast

The class is having a Thanksgiving feast that they prepare entirely by themselves. Adam, Joe, Lauren, and Kristi are in groups that are preparing mashed potatoes, cranberry sauce, corn, and pumpkin pie. Listen carefully to the clues and then draw a line connecting each person with what they will help prepare.

Clues

1. Adam and the boy helping with the cranberry sauce are working at tables next to each other.

2. Lauren and the girl helping make pumpkin pie agree that the room smells delicious.

3. Adam is not making the mashed potatoes.

Snack Time

Ron, Bob, Mary, and Sue brought different things for snack time. They brought a banana, an apple, raisins, and cookies. Listen carefully to the clues and then draw a line connecting each person with what they brought.

Clues

1. Ron and the boy with the apple sat together under a tree to eat their snacks.

2. Mary and the girl who brought raisins remembered to wash their hands before snack time.

3. Ron did not bring a banana.

Draw a line to the thing that should come next in each pattern.

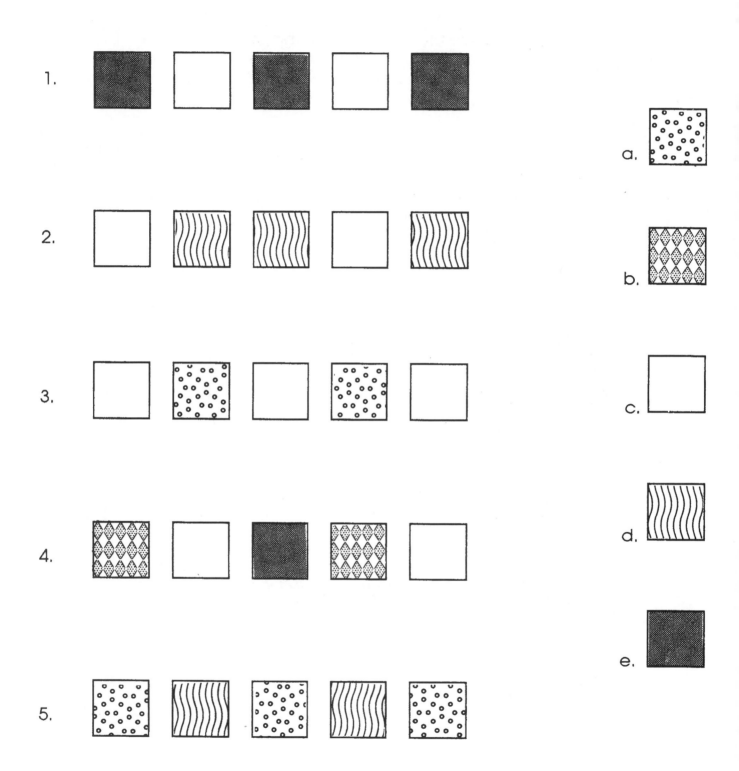

Draw a line to the thing that should come next in each pattern.

Draw a line to the thing that should come next in each pattern.

1.

2.

3.

4.

5.

a.

b.

c.

d.

Draw a line to the thing that should come next in each pattern.

1.

2.

3.

4.

5.

a.

b.

c.

d.

Draw a line to the thing that should come next in each pattern.

Draw a line to the thing that should come next in each pattern.

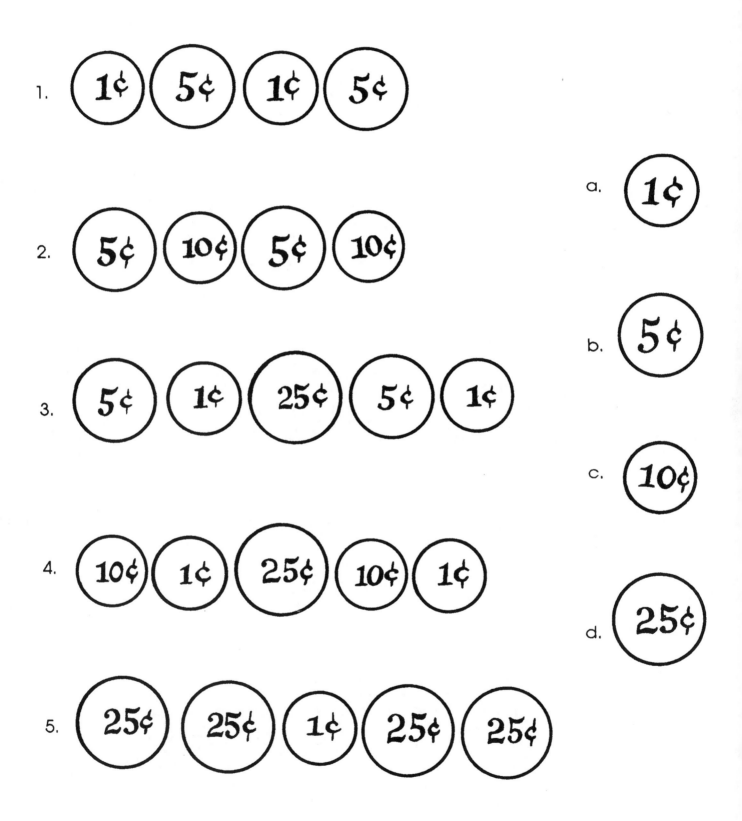

1. 1¢ 5¢ 1¢ 5¢

a. 1¢

2. 5¢ 10¢ 5¢ 10¢

b. 5¢

3. 5¢ 1¢ 25¢ 5¢ 1¢

c. 10¢

4. 10¢ 1¢ 25¢ 10¢ 1¢

d. 25¢

5. 25¢ 25¢ 1¢ 25¢ 25¢

Draw a line to the thing that should come next in each pattern.

1.

2.

a.

3.

b.

4.

c.

5.

d.

Draw a line to the thing that should come next in each pattern.

1.

2.

3.

4.

5.

a.

b.

c.

d.

Draw a line between each picture and the piece that would fit with it to make a complete picture.

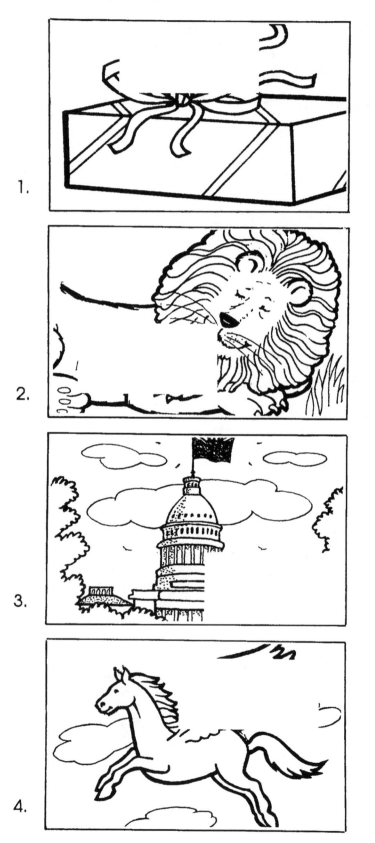

1.

2.

3.

4.

a.

b.

c.

d.

Draw a line between each picture and the piece that would fit with it to make a complete picture.

1.

2.

3.

4.

a.

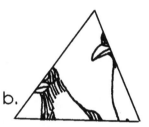

b.

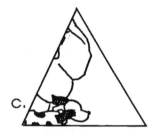

c.

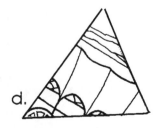

d.

Find the correct missing piece to complete each picture. Draw a circle around it.

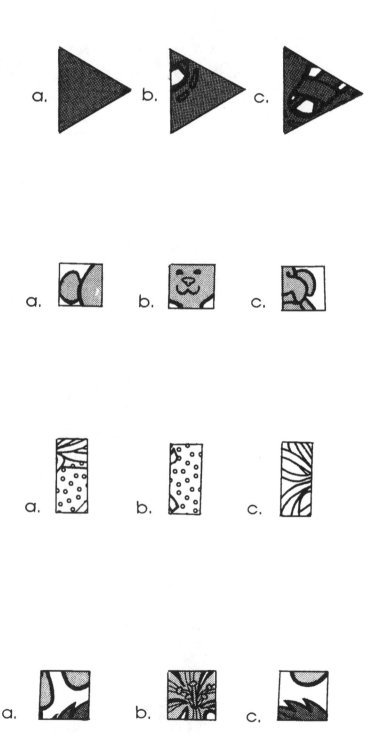

1.

a.   b.   c.

2.

a.   b.   c.

3.

a.   b.   c.

4.

a.   b.   c.

Find the correct missing piece to complete each picture. Draw a circle around it.

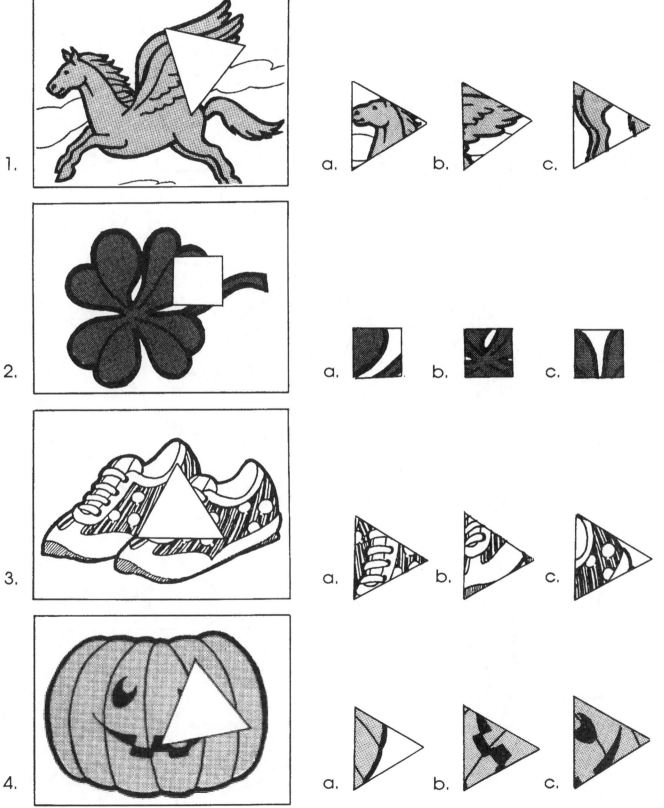

Look at the puzzle pieces. Decide what picture is on the puzzle. Draw it on another piece of paper.

Look at the puzzle pieces. Decide what picture is on the puzzle. Draw it on another piece of paper.

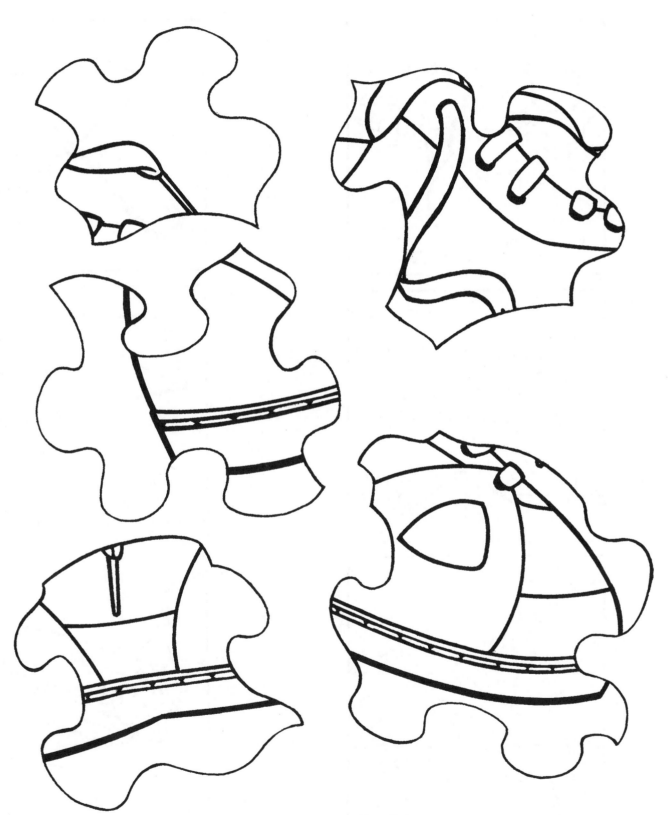

Draw a line to connect the pictures that go together.

Draw a line to connect the pictures that go together.

1.

a.

2.

b.

3.

c.

Can you guess what these pictures are?

1.

2.

3.

4.

Can you guess what these pictures are?

1.

2.

3.

4.

5.

6.

These are triops.

These are **not** triops.

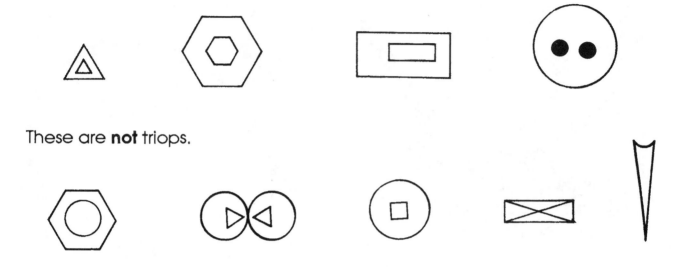

Draw a **circle** around all of these things that are triops. Draw an **X through** all the things that are not triops.

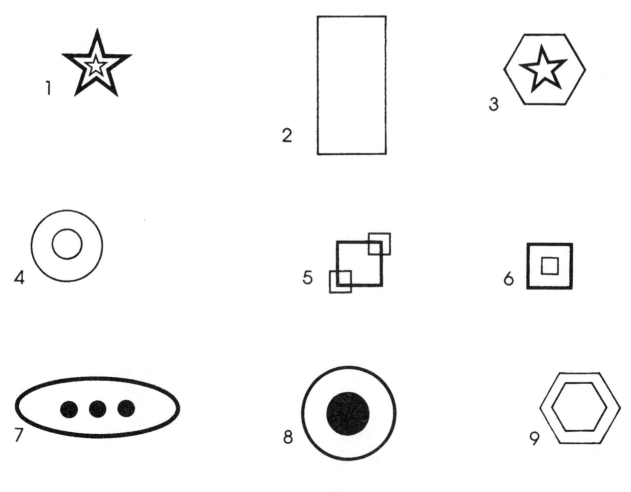

These are oggs.

These are **not** oggs.

Draw a **circle** around all of these things that are oggs. Draw an **X through** all the things that are not oggs.

These are tiffs.

These are **not** tiffs.

Draw a **circle** around all of these things that are tiffs. Draw an **X through** all the things that are not tiffs.

1
2
3
4
5
6

Answers

Lesson 1

1. e	2. d
3. c	4. f
5. a	6. b

Lesson 2

1. b	2. d
3. e	4. f
5. c	6. a

Lesson 3

1. f	2. d
3. a	4. e
5. b	6. c

Lesson 4

1. c	2. f
3. d	4. e
5. a	6. b

Lesson 5

1. a	2. f
3. b	4. c
5. d	6. e

Lesson 6

1. c	2. b
2. a	3. e
4. d	6. f

Lesson 7

1. f	2. b
3. c	4. d
5. e	6. a

Lesson 8

1. d	2. e
3. c	4. a
5. f	6. b

Lesson 9

1. b	2. b
3. c	4. a
5. b	

Lesson 10

1. b	2. c
3. c	4. b
5. a	

Lesson 11

1. b	2. a
3. c	4. a
5. b	

Lesson 12

1. a	2. b
3. a	4. c
5. b	

Lesson 13

circle 1, 2, 3, 5, 6, 9

Lesson 14

circle 4, 6, 7, 8, 10

Lesson 15

circle 4, 5, 6, 8, 9

Lesson 16

circle 2, 3, 6, 9

Lesson 17

1. c	2. a
3. b	4. c
5. b	

Lesson 18

1. b	2. a
3. c	4. c
5. b	

Lesson 19

1. a	2. c
3. c	4. b
5. b	

Lesson 20

1. b	2. c
3. c	4. a

Lesson 21

1. c	2. a
3. b	4. c

Lesson 22

1. b	2. c
3. a	4. c

Lesson 23

1. b	2. c
3. a	4. c

Lesson 24

1. b	2. c
3. a	4. b

Lesson 25
Pat - celery   Rob - onions
Ann - potatoes   Tom - carrots

Lesson 26
Ben - fire engine   Meg - hot-air balloon
John - helicopter   Diane - sail boat

Lesson 27
Luke - dog   Jill - fish
Pete - rabbit   Sara - cat

Lesson 28
Paul - sea shell   Amy - acorn
Matt - caterpillar   Chrissy - horseshoe

Lesson 29
Dan - pirate   Lisa - witch
Scott - cowboy   Kate - Cinderella

Lesson 30
Lauren - mashed potatoes   Adam - corn
Kristi - pumpkin pie   Joe - cranberry sauce

Lesson 31
Mary - banana   Ron - cookies
Sue - raisins   Bob - apple

Lesson 32
1. c   2. d
3. a   4. e
5. d

Lesson 33
1. c   2. g
3. a   4. e
5. e

Lesson 34
1. a   2. b
3. d   4. c
5. a

Lesson 35
1. c   2. d
3. b   4. d
5. a

Lesson 36
1. c   2. b
3. d   4. d
5. d

Lesson 37
1. a   2. b
3. d   4. d
5. a

Lesson 38
1. a   2. a
3. d   4. c
5. c

Lesson 39
1. b   2. d
3. c   4. a
5. c

Lesson 40
1. c   2. d
3. a   4. b

Lesson 41
1. b   2. d
3. a   4. c

Lesson 42
1. b   2. c
3. a   4. a

Lesson 43
1. b   2. a
3. a   4. c

Lesson 44
elephant

Lesson 45
shoe

Lesson 46
1. c   2. a
3. b

Lesson 47
1. b   2. c
3. a

Lesson 48
1. shoe   2. fish
3. pumpkin   4. turtle

Lesson 49
1. bird   2. pig
3. dinosaur   4. peice of pie
5. apple   6. skateboard

Lesson 50
circle 1, 4, 6, 8, 9

Lesson 51
circle 1, 2, 6

Lesson 52
circle 2, 3, 5

Lollipop Logic (Book 1)

Lesson	Common Core State Standards
Sequential Synthesis (Lessons 1-8)	Math: K.CC.A Know number names and the count sequence.
Relationships (Lessons 9-16)	ELA-Literacy: L.K.5 With guidance and support from adults, explore word relationships and nuances in word meanings. L.1.5 With guidance and support from adults, demonstrate understanding of word relationships and nuances in word meanings
Analogies (Lessons 17-24)	Math: K.G.B Analyze, compare, create, and compose shapes. 1.G.A & 2.G.A Reason with shapes and their attributes. ELA-Literacy: L.K.5 With guidance and support from adults, explore word relationships and nuances in word meanings. L.1.5 With guidance and support from adults, demonstrate understanding of word relationships and nuances in word meanings
Deductive Reasoning (Lessons 25-31)	ELA/Literacy: RF.K.1 & R.F.1.1 Demonstrate understanding of the organization and basic features of print. RF.K.3, R.F.1.3, & R.F.2.3 Know and apply grade-level phonics and word analysis skills in decoding words. R.F.1.4 & R.F.2.4 Read with sufficient accuracy and fluency to support comprehension.
Pattern Decoding (Lessons 32-39)	Math: 4.OA.C Generate and analyze patterns.
Critical Analyzing Skills (Lessons 50-52)	Math: K.CC.B Count to tell the number of objects. K.CC.C. Compare numbers. K.G.B Analyze, compare, create, and compose shapes. 1.G.A & 2.G.A Reason with shapes and their attributes.

Notes:
1. The standard addressed by the Pattern Decoding section of Lollipop Logic, Book 2, is listed as a fourth-grade Operations and Algebra standard by the CCSS. Although the concept of patterns may be addressed at a lower grade level, as it is in the activities in this section, the standard in this sheet reflects the first time it is covered in the CCSS.
2. Although the book was designed with the prereader in mind, the Deduction section includes clues and instructions that an early or emerging reader could read on his or her own to solve the activities, thus meeting the standards for Reading Foundations.